BOOKWORMS

Machines That Work

Big Cranes

Amy Hayes

Cavendish Square
New York

Published in 2016 by Cavendish Square Publishing, LLC
243 5th Avenue, Suite 136, New York, NY 10016

First Edition

CPSIA Compliance Information: Batch #WS15CSQ

Library of Congress Cataloging-in-Publication Data

Hayes, Amy.
Big cranes / Amy Hayes.
pages cm. — (Machines that work)
Includes index.
ISBN 978-1-50260-404-0 (hardcover) ISBN 978-1-50260-403-3 (paperback) ISBN 978-1-50260-405-7 (ebook)
1. Cranes, derricks, etc.—Juvenile literature. I. Title.
TJ1363.H38 2016
621.8'73—dc23
2015009756

Editorial Director: David McNamara
Copy Editor: Rebecca Rohan
Art Director: Jeff Talbot
Designer: Stephanie Flecha
Senior Production Manager: Jennifer Ryder-Talbot
Production Editor: Renni Johnson
Photo Research: J8 Media

The photographs in this book are used by permission and through the courtesy of: Image Source/Getty Images, cover; Alexandr Shevchenko/Shutterstock.com, 5; Richard Newstead/Moment/Getty Images, 7; Aleksey Sagitov/Shutterstock.com, 9; Eugene Sergeev/Shutterstock.com, 11; bogdanhoda/Shutterstock.com, 13; Zurijeta/Shutterstock.com, 15; Echo/Cultura/Getty Images, 17; LittleStocker/Shutterstock.com, 19; Corepics VOF/Shutterstock.com, 21.

Printed in the United States of America

Contents

Cranes are very tall!

Cranes have a long **mast** that reaches straight up high.

They have a **jib** that reaches far across.

Cranes have hooks that help them carry **loads**.

They can lift these
loads way up high!

Cranes help build buildings.

Cranes help load ships.

Some cranes are on ships!

Cranes are really **useful** machines.

New Words

jib (JIB) The side-to-side part of the crane that carries the load.

loads (LODES) Heavy things that are carried.

mast (MAST) The up-and-down part of the crane that makes it so tall.

useful (USE-full) Helpful.

Index

About the Author

Amy Hayes lives in the beautiful city of Buffalo, New York. She has written several books for children, including the Machines That Work and the Our Holidays series for Cavendish Square.

About BOOKWORMS

Bookworms help independent readers gain reading confidence through high-frequency words, simple sentences, and strong picture/text support. Each book explores a concept that helps children relate what they read to the world in which they live.